DATE DUE

5-19-05			
11-15-05			
11-28-05			
4-14-06			
12-21-07			
2-22-10			
5-27-10			

Demco, Inc. 38-293

Library

DOLPHINS

Melissa and Brandon Cole

BLACKBIRCH PRESS, INC.

WOODBRIDGE, CONNECTICUT

Published by Blackbirch Press, Inc.
260 Amity Road
Woodbridge, CT 06525

Email: staff@blackbirch.com
Web site: www.blackbirch.com

©2001 by Blackbirch Press, Inc.
First Edition

Printed in China

Photo Credits: All images ©Brandon D. Cole, except page 5: ©Gregory Ochocki.

10 9 8 7 6 5 4 3 2

Library of Congress Cataloging-in-Publication Data
Cole, Melissa S.
Dolphins / by Melissa S. Cole.
        p.   cm. — (Wild marine animals)
ISBN 1-56711-443-1   (hardcover : alk. paper)
1. Dolphins—Juvenile literature. [1. Dolphins.]   I. Title.
QL737.C432 C56 2001
599.53—dc21   2001000728

Contents

Introduction

Hector's dolphins swim together. These dolphins are the rarest and smallest in the world.

Long ago, people thought dolphins were fish. Now we know that dolphins are marine mammals. Like humans, cats, and all other mammals, these warm-blooded animals breathe air with lungs and nurse their young.

Dolphins live in many places. Some, such as the bottlenose dolphin and the common dolphin, are found in all the world's oceans. Spotted and spinner dolphins are found only in warm water. A few species, such as the Pacific white-sided dolphin, are found most often in cool oceans. The harbor porpoise and Hector's dolphin prefer the waters of the shallow coast. Extremely rare river dolphins are found living in some of the largest, muddiest, freshwater rivers in Asia and South America.

Amazon River dolphins live in the muddy rivers of South America.

Members of the Family

Dolphins are actually members of the same family as the gigantic sperm whale and the orca (killer whale). There are more than 30 species in this animal family, which is known to scientists as the "cetaceans." Here are descriptions of just a few of the more common species of dolphins.

Bottlenose Dolphins

Bottlenose dolphins are found in the warm areas of most oceans. They are the most common species kept in zoos and aquariums. Some bottlenoses weigh up to 1,000 pounds (454 kilograms) and reach nearly 13 feet (4 meters) in length.

A group of spotted dolphins swims in the Atlantic Ocean. The younger dolphins are gray.

Spotted Dolphins

Spotted dolphins are found in temperate and tropical oceans. Baby spotted dolphins are born without spots, which appear as these dolphins grow older.

Common Dolphins

Common dolphins usually swim together in large groups. They are easy to recognize by the hourglass pattern and yellow patches on their bodies. They have long, thin snouts called beaks with sharp, pointed teeth.

Porpoises, like this Dall's porpoise, have blunt beaks and small dorsal fins.

Pacific White-Sided Dolphins

These dolphins are mainly found in the cool waters of the Northern Pacific Ocean. They often travel together in large groups called herds. They have dark backs, light sides, and very short beaks.

Porpoises

Porpoises are similar to dolphins, although they are often smaller. They have blunt beaks and spade-shaped teeth instead of the conical or cone-shaped teeth of a dolphin.

The Body of a Dolphin

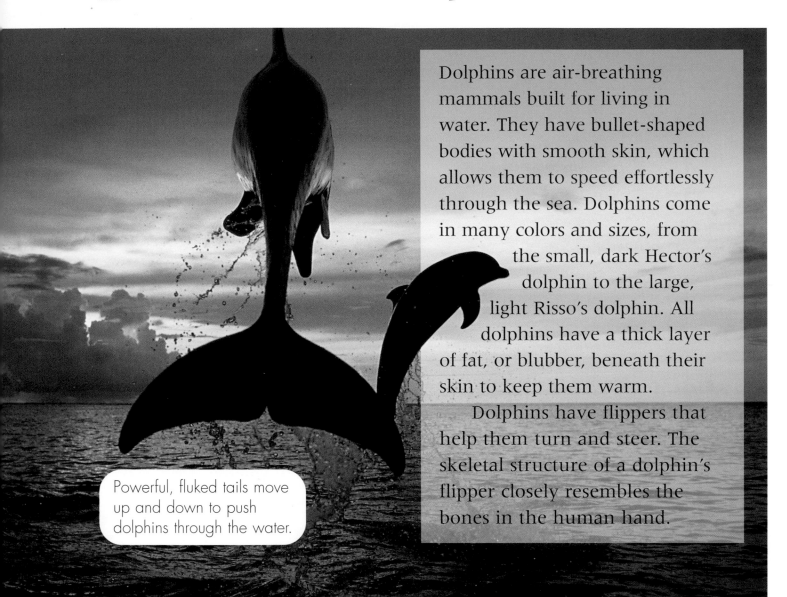

Dolphins are air-breathing mammals built for living in water. They have bullet-shaped bodies with smooth skin, which allows them to speed effortlessly through the sea. Dolphins come in many colors and sizes, from the small, dark Hector's dolphin to the large, light Risso's dolphin. All dolphins have a thick layer of fat, or blubber, beneath their skin to keep them warm.

Dolphins have flippers that help them turn and steer. The skeletal structure of a dolphin's flipper closely resembles the bones in the human hand.

Powerful, fluked tails move up and down to push dolphins through the water.

Sharp, cone-shaped teeth, help dolphins hold slippery prey.

Scientists think dolphins evolved from a group of small, furry mammals that used to feed along the water's edge.

Most dolphins have a large, curved dorsal fin on their back that helps them balance and stay upright in the water. Instead of hind legs, dolphins have powerful, fluked tails. Their tails move up and down, not side to side like a fish's tail. A dolphin tail has two flukes that act like a paddle to help push the animal through the water.

Dolphins use their snouts or beaks to catch slippery fish and squid. Some species of dolphins have only 8 teeth, while others have as many as 250! Males usually have more teeth than females.

Special Features

Dolphins have many special features that help them live in their watery world. Dolphins breathe through a special feature called a blowhole. A blowhole is like a nostril on top of a dolphin's head. The dolphin takes a breath through its blowhole at the surface and the hole seals tight when the dolphin goes underwater. This allows dolphins to use air as they swim underwater. It also means dolphins don't need to lift their heads out of the water to get their next breath.

Behind a dolphin's upper jaw is a bulgy "forehead" of fatty tissue called a melon. Inside this melon is a series of air tubes. Dolphins use these air tubes to make chirping and squeaking sounds by squeezing air from one cavity to another.

Dolphins breathe through blowholes on top of their heads.

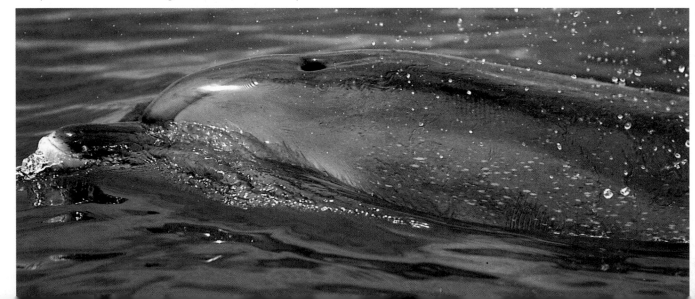

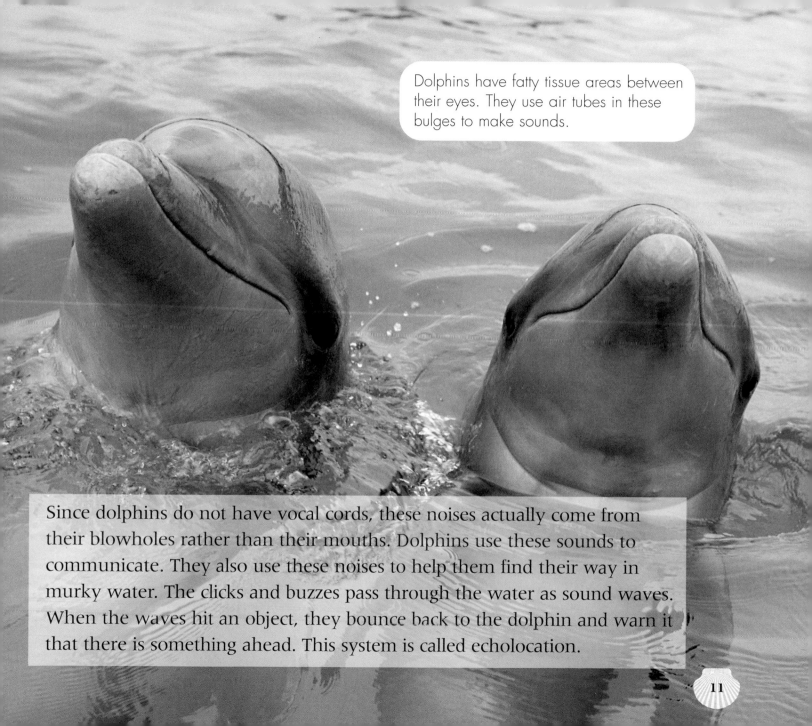

Dolphins have fatty tissue areas between their eyes. They use air tubes in these bulges to make sounds.

Since dolphins do not have vocal cords, these noises actually come from their blowholes rather than their mouths. Dolphins use these sounds to communicate. They also use these noises to help them find their way in murky water. The clicks and buzzes pass through the water as sound waves. When the waves hit an object, they bounce back to the dolphin and warn it that there is something ahead. This system is called echolocation.

In captivity, dolphins have been trained to perform a wide variety of tricks and feats.

Echolocation is especially useful to river dolphins, who are practically blind. Good eyesight is useless in muddy river water where visibility is poor. Instead, these dolphins use echolocation that creates a "sound picture" and "describes" the surroundings.

Many dolphins have light-colored bellies and dark-colored backs. This type of camouflage helps them blend into their habitat. Looking down at dolphins from above, they are almost invisible against the dark, ocean depths. When seen from below, they are difficult to make out against the brightness of the surface waters.

One of the most important features of dolphins is their incredible intelligence. In captivity, they have shown they are quick to learn tricks.

Some even teach tricks to their dolphin friends! Dolphins have been trained by the military to find missing people, as well as to locate explosives. Wild dolphins use their smarts to find food, hunt for prey in new ways, and avoid predators, such as sharks, orcas, and even humans. Every day, researchers learn more about dolphin behaviors and communication. Maybe one day humans will actually be able to understand what dolphins are saying!

Light-colored bellies help dolphins blend in to their surroundings when seen from below.

Social Life

Dolphins travel in large groups.

Dolphins are social animals that touch each other and rub their bodies together. They play games with "toys" such as seaweed, pebbles, and fish. They throw them into the air, carry them around in their mouths, balance them on their flippers, and pass them to one another. They often chase each other, leaping into the air, splashing their flukes, and rolling over. Many dolphins enjoy riding in the bow waves of boats and ships. When they hear the humming of an engine, they swim over as fast as they can.

Dolphins usually live together in groups. The size of the group depends on the species. For example, bottlenose and spotted dolphins usually live in

Dolphins are social animals that enjoy touching each other.

small groups of about ten. Common and Pacific white-sided dolphins live in huge herds, sometimes number-ing in the thousands. Within a herd, the dolphins tend to group together by age and sex. Females with calves or babies form one group while juveniles or young form another. Adult males usually make up a third group. When the herd is threatened, mothers and babies move toward the center and are protected by large males and females without calves. Dolphins can use their beaks to give a strong blow like a punch to the soft bellies of their predators. They have even been known to kill sharks when attacked!

One of the most amazing things about dolphins is the way they commu-nicate. Every dolphin has its own voice—a special whistling sound called a signature whistle. This is like a name, and it identifies an individual dolphin. Dolphin groups constantly whistle to each other to help them stay close together.

Hunting and Food

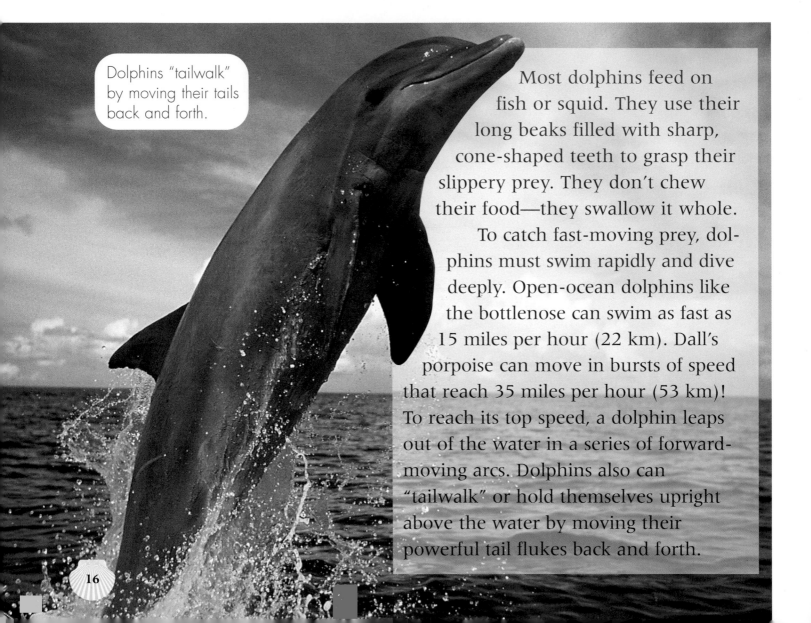

Dolphins "tailwalk" by moving their tails back and forth.

Most dolphins feed on fish or squid. They use their long beaks filled with sharp, cone-shaped teeth to grasp their slippery prey. They don't chew their food—they swallow it whole. To catch fast-moving prey, dolphins must swim rapidly and dive deeply. Open-ocean dolphins like the bottlenose can swim as fast as 15 miles per hour (22 km). Dall's porpoise can move in bursts of speed that reach 35 miles per hour (53 km)! To reach its top speed, a dolphin leaps out of the water in a series of forward-moving arcs. Dolphins also can "tailwalk" or hold themselves upright above the water by moving their powerful tail flukes back and forth.

Dolphins use acrobatics to find prey. For example, by jumping into the air or tail walking, a dolphin can scan the surface of the ocean and look for seabirds feeding on schools of fish near the surface.

Some species of dolphins travel with the seasons to follow large schools of fish or squid. Off the coast of California, bottlenose dolphins can be seen migrating south every autumn and returning north every spring.

When chasing fish, dolphins may use their melons to make bursts of high-frequency sounds. These powerful sound waves can kill fish. Dolphins also use echolocation to find fish hiding beneath the sand. After they find the fish, they use their long beaks to dig them out.

Although they are called "killer whales," orcas are actually the largest members of the dolphin family. Some orcas feed mainly on fish. Other orcas roam the sea and feed on animals, such as seals, dolphins, turtles, and even other whales. These whales, called transient orcas, hunt like a pack of wolves. They surround their prey and work as a team to capture it.

Long beaks help dolphins dig out fish beneath the sand.

The Mating Game

Scientific research shows that dolphins can live for a long time. Bottlenose males live into their forties. Females often survive into their fifties. Females usually begin giving birth between the ages of five and six. A female will have a single calf about once every three years. She usually mates with more than one male. Males often are quite aggressive towards each other when they are competing for a female's attention. Many males have "rake marks" on their skin, which come from the teeth of competing males. After mating, males usually leave the group and move on. When a female gives birth, the father dolphin plays no part in raising the young calf.

"Rake marks" on skin and fins are from the teeth of competing males.

Some kinds of dolphins can live to be forty or fifty years old.

Raising Young

Young dolphins stay with their mothers for several years.

Female dolphins are pregnant for about twelve months. When it is born, a baby bottlenose is close to 3 feet (1 meter) long and shaped a bit like a football! At first, its fins, flukes, and flippers are quite rubbery. This helps make the birth easier because nothing gets caught on the way out. The fins stiffen within a few days.

Dolphins are born underwater, close to the surface. Another female dolphin called an "aunt" may help the mother during birth. She also cares for the baby in the early months.

When a calf is born, it often comes out tail first. A newborn calf has no air in its lungs. As soon as it is free it begins to sink. The mother and "aunt" immediately nudge the baby towards the surface to take its first breath. Within about 30 minutes, it can swim on its own.

A baby begins to nurse soon after birth. While the mother lies on her side, they both hold their breath as the baby gulps milk that squirts into its mouth from the mother.

A newborn spotted dolphin swims close to its mother.

Bottlenose calves feed on their mother's milk for up to 18 months. A dolphin's milk has a high fat content, which helps babies grow rapidly. When they are about six months old, young dolphins usually have their first taste of fish. They nibble on scraps left behind after the adults have hunted. As the young dolphins grow older, they grow teeth and learn to hunt on their own.

The strongest bond of all is the one between a mother and her calf. A young dolphin stays with its mom for up to two or three years.

Dolphins and Humans

Many people enjoy watching dolphins in the wild.

Dolphins have enchanted humans ever since the first fishermen went to sea. We admire their speed and grace, and we are fascinated by their intelligence.

Some people believe dolphins can heal the sick. No one knows how it works, but autistic children—who have trouble interacting with the world around them—seem to respond to contact with dolphins.

Though many people love dolphins, humans are the dolphin's chief enemy. In some parts of the world, fishermen use enormous nets—called drift nets—up to 30 miles (48 kilometers) long. The nets are practically invisible, and as they drift through the sea, dolphins become trapped. These animals often drown because they are unable to swim to the surface. In the last 30 years, about 7 million dolphins have drowned in large nets. Nets with dolphin "escape hatches" have recently decreased the numbers of netted dolphins, but thousands are still killed every year.

Another threat from humans is pollution. Chemicals from industrial wastes, oil, sewage, and pesticides often end up in the ocean. These poisons are stored in body fat, and because dolphins have thick layers of fat, chemicals can build up in their tissues and make them sick.

For centuries, humans have enjoyed a unique bond with dolphins. We have been captivated by the possibility of actually communicating with them. That, however, will never happen if we don't work hard to preserve these animals and protect the watery world in which they live.

Snorkelers can sometimes swim within inches of curious dolphins.

GLOSSARY

blubber The fat under the skin of a whale, seal, or dolphin.

camouflage Covering or coloring that makes animals, people, and objects look like their surroundings.

habitat The place and natural condition in which a plant or animal lives.

prey An animal that is hunted by another animal for food.

species A group of similar animals.

FOR MORE INFORMATION

Books

Brust, Beth Wagner. *Dolphins and Porpoises* (Zoobooks). Mankato, MN: Creative Education, 2000.

Carwardine, Mark. *Whales, Dolphins, and Porpoises* (See and Explore). New York: Dorling Kindersley, 1998.

Davies, Nicola. *Dolphin: Habitats, Life Cycles, Food Chains, Threats* (Natural World). Chatham, NJ: Raintree/Steck Vaughn, 2000.

Walker, Sally M. *Dolphins* (Nature Watch). Minneapolis, MN: Carolrhoda Books, 1999.

Web Site

Ultimate Guide: Dolphins

Learn more interesting dolphin facts as well as find out what different dolphin sounds mean—
www.discovery.com/stories/nature/dolphins/dolphins.html

INDEX